Resilience

THE STRENGTH OF A WOMAN

"Accountability Affirmations to Transform Your Life"

ASHLEY NICOLE

Dedication

This book is dedicated to my two beautiful daughters, Brooke and Draya. Becoming a mother lit a fire under me that I don't believe a match could have done. You two are my heart and the reason I have super-powers. The love I have for you ladies is insurmountable. I have sacrificed many things because of such love, and I would not trade the bond that we have for the world. Without you two, I would not know my strengths or my weaknesses. I would not know the depths of my capabilities, nor would I be forced to exercise the drive and determination that is within me to provide you with a pleasurable childhood. I am grateful to be your mother. I love you so much!

I would also like to dedicate this gem to my Aunt Linda...the strongest woman I know. You labored until your very last breath. I watched you endure a lot with minimal complaints. You will always be my hero.

Lastly, I would like to dedicate this book to all of the women around the world who are trying...who are sacrificing...who sit in the garage for a few minutes before walking into the house...who cry in the shower...who overcome silent battles never spoken of. This book was written with you in mind.

Table of Contents

Introduction

Who encourages the encourager? Who encourages the strong man? There will be many times when it will only be you and the God that lives within you to get you through the day. We don't just wake up and decide to have a bad day. Oftentimes, we wake up carrying the burdens we've encountered throughout life...unaddressed childhood issues, relational trauma, environmental circumstances, and everything else that comes with life. This book is designed to affirm and reaffirm your God-intended creation...to assist you with declaring God's destiny and purpose over your life. This book was created to spread joy, love, and, most importantly, peace. This book is also designed to provoke perspective in a way that your psychological construct has never seen before. By proposing and declaring these affirmations, your spirit man should respond, causing you to take a different approach in decision-making that will ultimately put you in the driver's seat of your life. You and the holy spirit within you are responsible for your own happiness and holistic well-being.

How To Use

In order to reap the full benefits that come with this book, intentionality is necessary. You must be intentional with your time-management skills, creating space and an atmosphere to meditate (think deeply or focus one's mind for a period of time) on the words you declare over your day and, ultimately, your life. Make sure that you understand the meaning of every word in which you read. Most importantly, you must open your mind, body, and spirit to change. You must be willing to surrender your thoughts and ideas to that which is guided by God. It won't be easy, but the journey will be well worth it.

Chapter 1:
Grief

Whether through death or failed relationships, many of us have experienced grief in some form. I remember when my aunt passed away from cancer. We were really close and would talk during my morning commutes to work. My aunt was my hero. She built her basement with her own hands and money. She would cut grass and work a full-time job with no complaints. Even up to her passing, she was still trying to work.

When she passed away, I did not attend the funeral because of the pain I knew that I would endure, just knowing that she would no longer be able to call me in the mornings. She left behind young children and grandchildren. In order to better deal with the pain, I began to celebrate the life of my aunt.

I worked harder with her in mind. If I felt like complaining, I thought about her because my aunt did so much without complaints. The pain seemed manageable when I began to carry her with me throughout my life. I learned that instead of keeping your loved ones as memories, take them with you. The pain seems more bearable, and their life becomes celebratory throughout your journey.

Loss by way of a divorce or break-up can be tricky. Depending on the cause of the separation, one's emotions can be high and all over the place. As a result, the journey through the five stages of grief could intensify. These five stages include: Denial, anger, bargaining, depression, and acceptance. Unfortunately, once one has gone through this grief process, the residue of sadness is still present.

While going through my first divorce, yes, first... there were two. I felt like I failed. I felt like I let myself down, and God and my children were included. Despite being given clear instructions from the holy spirit that I'd been released from the marriage, I still remembered the vows. It made me feel like a hypocrite. The first thing I knew I had to do was forgive myself for failing. I began to climb my way out of such negative mental spaces by being intentional about reflecting and learning about the things that went on in the marriage.

I began questioning myself as to why I chose my husband at the time. I would ask myself, "Why did you ignore the red flags" and "What made him enough at the time." I considered my age and situation during our courtship. I really wanted to learn my "why" to get to the root of my decisions. After being intentional about learning more about myself through this reflection process, I was able to get more of an understanding of who I was and what I wanted in the future. I began to ask God to give me the strength to let go. I asked God to bring clarity and peace to my spirit and my life.

I spent many days with God because I knew he wouldn't let me down. I needed the strength of the holy spirit to begin a work in me so that I would not be bitter, angry, mad, or resentful. I wanted to co-parent effectively and with love for the sake of my daughters. I knew that I did not want this loss to affect my children to the magnitude that it would sow seeds of rejection or instability. So, as a mother, I forgave and took strides to compromise and even sacrifice for the sake of a peaceful environment among my now ex-husband, myself, and our daughters. I chose to walk in love no matter the circumstances.

As a result, I felt formidable. I'm glad that I decided to walk in love because a few years later, my ex-husband passed away. A feeling of peace comes over me when I think about our relationship post-marriage. I made a choice. The right choice to forgive and release.

<u>Scripture Focus</u>

Psalm 34:18

"The Lord is close to the brokenhearted and saves those who are crushed in spirit."

Psalm 147:3

"He heals the brokenhearted and binds up their wounds."

With <u>faith</u> and <u>confidence</u>, declare these affirmations over your life:

- *Because I am your creation, I trust you, God, with my whole heart.*
- *I trust that you are near to me. I know that in my weakness, you are made strong. I am your child, and without you, I can do nothing.*
- *I will trust that in time that God will heal my*

wounds because he is near to the brokenhearted.

- *Rather than grieve in sorrow, I will strive daily to celebrate those whom I miss dearly.*
- *I will cherish the memories through laughter.*
- *I understand that I may never get over the loss, but rather carry those whom I miss near to my heart.*
- *With God, I can do all things.*
- *I will lean on God when I am weak.*
- *God bottles up my tears because he cares for me.*
- *I will be intentional to show love to my loved ones while I have the opportunity.*
- *I will forgive quickly.*
- *I will not become a victim of grief.*
- *I choose joy and an abundant life.*

Chapter 2:
Trauma-Triggers

As we greet each morning, we have daily routines that we implement throughout the day. However, there is always room for the unknown to occur...unknown encounters, unknown emotions, unknown accidents, unknown upsets, unknown disappointments, unknown opportunities, unknown good moments, and unknown bad moments. Each of these unknown entities makes way for triggers to occur.

A trigger is a response caused by a particular action. Triggers are attached to trauma of any sort. They can shape your very being. They can dictate your social life in ways that significantly impact your personality and interactions with others. Triggers are more prevalent in relationships. They are often identified through emotional reactions derived from a person, place, thing, or situation.

One must first identify her triggers and confront the root of the trigger head-on. This is the first step to healing. We cannot be healthy and whole without addressing our emotional trauma and triggers. In addition, we cannot expect to acquire healthy relationships without addressing our triggers. I must admit that I didn't realize I had triggers until my emotional response was something other than what I expected. I can remember being on the phone with a friend who was experiencing the same health symptoms as my first husband experienced, and these symptoms ultimately caused my first husband's death. I remember in the midst of explaining what my first husband experienced, my breath was taken from me, and I began to have a complete meltdown.

I was so embarrassed and shocked because I could not understand where such a burst of emotions had come from. After all, it had been five years since my first husband's passing. As I reflected, I realized that I had not properly grieved his death. You would be surprised at what you unconsciously carry around. Such unaddressed grief can easily grow into sadness and depression if not dealt with appropriately.

Many adults have unhealed adolescent trauma. These traumas include abuse, neglect, molestation, abandonment, etc. Such traumas can show up in relationships and how you deal with others. These traumas can be the root of one's inability to communicate appropriately, personality flaws, untamed relational habits, isolation, and the inability to rationalize emotions properly.

Traumas also manifest in the body. Examples of physical trauma manifestations are obesity, anxiety, depression, and tension headaches. In order to tackle these traumas and triggers, one must seek Godly counsel through prayer and obtain some counseling and/or therapy. Some would say that if you can be triggered, then you are not healed. Please understand that healing is a process, and we must be patient with ourselves. We must learn coping skills to better deal with our triggers so that they do not control our lives.

Scripture Focus:

Psalm 91:4-6

"He will cover you with his feathers, and under his wings you will find refuge; his faithfulness will be your shield and rampart. You will not fear the terror of night, nor the arrow that flies by day, nor the pestilence that stalks in the darkness, nor the plague that destroys at midday."

With <u>faith</u> and <u>confidence</u>, declare these affirmations over your life:

- *I will not let past traumas produce conflict in my communication with others.*
- *I am allowing myself to feel and acknowledge all unpleasant emotions and develop a coping strategy.*
- *My past does not define me.*
- *I will not let past traumas create difficulty within my relationships.*

- *I am allowing space in my heart for the forgiveness of those who have hurt me.*
- *I will be cognizant of any negative energy around me because it is detrimental to my healing.*
- *I will not let past traumas control my parenting skills.*
- *I will maintain control of my emotions.*
- *I release the past and trust that good things are happening to me.*
- *I am a generational curse breaker.*
- *I am more than a conqueror through Jesus Christ.*
- *Greater is HE that is in me, than he that is in the world.*
- *I will be intentional about loving ALL of myself.*
- *I am taking actions today that my future self would be proud of.*

Chapter 3:
Mental Health

What do you think of when you hear the words "mental health?" Do you think of an illness of some sort, or do you think of the state of health within your mind? Hopefully, it is the latter. Women wear soooo many hats in the world today; it's a wonder why all of us have not entirely shut down as a species. All of us wear at least one of these crowns...we are mothers, entrepreneurs, wives, sisters, daughters, employees, caretakers, students, or all at once.

A woman's role on this earth is heavily weighted. There are what seems like a million responsibilities and not enough time in one day. Because women are stretched thin, it is imperative that we make our mental health a priority. If our mental health is not intact, then we don't get to fulfill the aforementioned responsibilities that come with wearing such crowns in a loving and healthy manner. We don't get to enjoy the opportunity to take care of the ones that we love the most. We must be cautious not to let depression, anxiety, and just plain old exhaustion creep into our bodies. It is our responsibility to take care of ourselves holistically. Because everything starts within the mind, we must pay close attention to our thought processes, our emotions, and our bodies. While anxiety's origin is psychological, it can manifest physically. Self-awareness is key. One has to be able to identify when she is exhausted, depressed, or anxious.

It was only just a few years ago that I conquered my battle with depression. I like to isolate myself, which can be a clear indicator;

however, my personality enjoys alone time. I overcame depression when I discovered my triggers. In order to discover such triggers, I became aware of my surroundings and atmosphere. I was intentional during a depressed state and often asked myself, "What triggered this?" Other times, I would evaluate my space and realize that there was too much clutter. It is true that your mind is a representation of your space. I realized that I needed clean spaces that included sunlight and refreshing aromas.

I am also careful about the things that I watch on television, specifically reality tv, which includes drama. We all know that drama supports and intensifies negative behavior. In addition, I do not watch much news because of the sadness that it could trigger within our reality. I am also careful about the type of conversations I have, steering clear of gossip and negative conversations with friends and family. These things seep into your mental space causing unconscious negativity. It is an unconscious weight on your mental health when you step into the seat of negative conversations and engage in activity that involves negative energy. No person who battles depression and/or anxiety should expose themselves to such negative and toxic environments. The ultimate goal is to obtain joy, peace, love, and contentment, creating a positive atmosphere and achieving a positive mindset.

In order to achieve a positive mindset, boundaries must be implemented. One must enforce boundaries to self-preserve one's mental health. Boundaries are those which separate your physical space, needs, feelings, and responsibilities from others. Boundaries also tell and teach others how to treat you. It is extremely important that you know all of yourself so that you can establish boundaries sufficient for your mental health. You cannot set proper boundaries without knowing your limitations holistically. Think about what causes that feeling of anxiousness or overwhelming frustration, then set your boundaries so that these feelings can be prevented.

Boundaries are a proactive way to get ahead of what could easily be turbulence in your life. Effective ways to set healthy boundaries include: Identifying your limits, openly communicating your boundaries, not being afraid to say no, upholding your boundaries, and taking time for yourself.

Scripture Focus

Matthew 11:28-30

"Come to me, all you who are weary and burdened, and I will give you rest.   Take my yoke upon you and learn from me, for I am gentle and humble in heart, and you will find rest for souls. For my yoke is easy, and my burden is light."

With <u>faith</u> and <u>confidence</u>, declare these affirmations over your life:

- *I can do ALL things through Christ who strengthens me.*
- *I will cast down every negative thought and imagination that exalts itself above who God says I am.*
- *I will not let depression, anxiety, or any other tormenting mental spirit consume my thoughts.*

- *I will communicate my feelings in a healthy manner.*
- *I will learn to say "no" and/or "not now."*
- *I will approach the day with a positive mindset.*
- *I will replace negative thoughts with positive thoughts.*
- *I control my thoughts, and today my thoughts are free and positive.*
- *I let go of anything and anyone that does not have my best interest at heart.*
- *I will protect my peace at all times.*
- *I will set boundaries within my relationships between family and friends that protect my peace.*
- *I will implement strategic daily routines that will serve my peace.*

Chapter 4:
Self-Care

n the previous chapter, we discussed boundaries to safeguard your mental health. Boundaries are also a form of self-care. I cannot stress how important it is as a woman to know ALL of who you are... mind, body, and spirit, so that you can identify what boundaries work best for you. Boundaries focus on the negative forces that can disrupt exciting and fulfilling moments.

Think on these things. What is it that you enjoy doing for yourself? What makes you inclusively happy? What are your hobbies? What are your goals? Have you discovered your purpose? Notice I have not asked you anything that pertains to things you dislike. This is because self-care focuses on activities that bring about enjoyment and pleasure. You have to be able to identify self-care activities that are pleasing to you. On the contrary, you also have to be able to discern the people, places, and things that can interrupt such activities. If you cannot properly identify that which brings a halt to your self-care, you cannot set a proper boundary.

So why is self-care important? Self-care is essential because we have to be whole and operate as our best selves. We want to achieve the best versions of ourselves so that we can create the most pleasurable experiences with and for our loved ones. Let's admit it, ladies; when we are going through a bad breakup or tough times, we are frustrated and irritable. As a result, our loved ones don't experience the best moments with us.

One thing that I have no problem admitting

is that I filed for divorce BOTH times, and the driving factor was not necessarily an act of betrayal. It was knowing how miserable I would be if I stayed in those marriages. I knew that I could not achieve my best version while dealing with such disappointments, torment, and frustration that derived from the betrayal. I knew that I could not give my daughters their best mother. That alone is enough for me to get out of a toxic relationship and/or situation.   Making this decision called for me to set boundaries like no other and ultimately achieve the highest form of self-care...my self-respect, my dignity, and my peace...crown me.

When a woman is able to take care of herself holistically, she gains liberation. She gains power. She gains strength.   She achieves the confidence needed to acquire success in any arena she chooses. She can see her vision through and execute it. She understands who God is in her life as well as the reciprocity needed to maintain such a vertical relationship with Him. She operates in an apex mentality...she has reached the highest and best version of herself, so much so that she is not threatened by another woman or that woman's happiness and achievements. She is able to celebrate another woman because she has gained happiness and wholeness on her own.

Scripture Focus:

3 John 1:2-4

"Dear friend, I pray that you may enjoy good health and that all may go well with you, even as your soul is getting along well.   It gave me great joy when some believers came and testified about your faithfulness to the truth, telling how you continue to walk in it. I have no greater joy than to hear that my children are walking in the truth."

1 Corinthians 3:16-17

"Don't you know that you yourselves are God's temple and that God's Spirit dwells in your midst? If anyone destroys God's temple, God will destroy that person; for God's temple is sacred, and you together are that temple."

Proverbs 4:23

"Above all else, guard your heart, for everything you do flows from it."

With <u>faith</u> and <u>confidence</u>, declare these affirmations over your life:

- *I am thankful for the beautiful life that I am creating.*
- *I appreciate the woman that I am becoming.*
- *I have many great qualities.*
- *I love my life and everyone in it.*
- *I love my circle of positive people.*
- *I set boundaries to remain spiritually and emotionally sound.*
- *I am cognizant of atmospheres that do not serve positivity.*
- *I am intentional about taking care of myself...mind, body, and spirit.*
- *My body is my temple.*

- *I make my health a priority.*
- *I am intentional about sticking to my goals.*
- *I am consistent with the goals that I have set in order to achieve growth.*
- *I will place no limitations on my growth.*
- *I take pride in my appearance.*
- *I take pride in my accomplishments and reward myself as I see fit.*
- *I am determined to achieve a better version of myself.*
- *Because I set healthy boundaries, I can thrive in mental euphoria.*
- *Greater is He that is in me than He that is in the world.*

Chapter 5:
The Single Mother

A woman rarely chooses to be a single parent. In fact, most of us made the choice of parenting with the notion that the other party would automatically fill the obligation of rising to the occasion as needed. Unfortunately, this is not always the case. Being a single parent is one of the most mentally and physically challenging titles an individual can have. If you are not careful, those challenges can get the best of you. The never-ending challenges that come with single parenting come with exhaustion. If one has no support from family and/or friends, it will cause you to feel isolated and alone. Such isolation is the breeding ground for depression and loneliness.

I remember when I found out that I was pregnant with my first child. I was in my last semester of college, with a part-time job and no husband.   My high-school boyfriend and I moved in together during my four-year tenure in college. We were both unestablished. When things did not work out, I found myself single with a new baby and soooo much pressure.

There were many, many days I cried during my morning commute to work, thinking about how I was going to take care of this child by myself.   I had no family in the area and no real local support outside of a few friends here and there.   I was forced to make a choice. Allow this situation to weigh me down or allow this situation to be the catalyst that would thrust me into being the best mother and woman that I could possibly be. After all, I did not want my child to witness or endure the hardships that I faced as a child.

I made a decision. I chose LIFE! I knew it would not be easy, but the love that was placed on the inside of me for this child would not let me quit. I focused on myself and not her father. I made it my business to provide at all costs for her. I developed a determination so strong that no failed relationship, no financial hardship, and no setback of any sort would deter me from "securing the bag" for my child and her future. I lived a life with minimal excuses and many sacrifices. Hard work requires discipline and obedience. I began to grow in my faith and relied heavily on the scriptures and the spirit of GOD to carry me through. After 17 years, I can proudly say that my daughter lives a rather attractive teenage lifestyle. When I see the fruit of my labor, it makes every laborious tear worth it.

I want to encourage every woman reading this that if God graced the female species to endure the labor pains with the ability to not only carry life but give life, he would not cause such life to create a dead situation of loneliness without providing and making a way for you to care for your child. God is ALWAYS with you. If you trust that He is your source and increase your faith and spirit being, you will find resilience on the other side of your victory!

What is resilience? Resilience is having the ability to withstand or recover quickly from difficult conditions. It is the ability to spring back into shape after bending, stretching (like we do after childbirth), or compression. In other words, resilience is the ability to bounce back from hard times. This is why knowing who you are in Christ is extremely important. You have to know that while you may be physically alone, God is with you, providing, leading, and protecting you every step of the way. Faith teaches us to trust not solely in our own abilities but rather in God's ability. Always remember that God can do anything but fail!

Scripture focus

Isaiah 43:2

"When you pass through the waters, I will be with you; and when you pass through the rivers, they will not sweep over you.   When you walk through the fire, you will not be burned; the flames will not set you ablaze."

Romans 8:18

"I consider that our present sufferings are not worth comparing with the glory that will be revealed in us."

Psalm 23:4

"Even though I walk through the darkest valley, I will fear no evil, for you are with me; your rod and your staff, they comfort me.

With <u>faith</u> and <u>confidence</u>, declare these affirmations over your life:

- *I am never alone because God walks with me.*
- *God will never leave me nor forsake me.*
- *I trust that God will supply all of my needs.*
- *There is nothing too hard for God.*
- *I will not worry because my faith is in my creator.*
- *I will use my pain to fuel my destiny.*
- *I am grateful for the opportunities that are before me.*
- *I can do all things through Christ, who gives me strength.*
- *I believe in myself.*
- *I refuse to give up.*
- *I am courageous.*
- *I am a fighter.*
- *I can overcome anything that I put my mind*

to.

- *I am not letting my bad decisions consume me with sadness and worry.*
- *I am learning from my mistakes daily.*
- *I will triumph.*
- *I am creating a healthy and loving atmosphere for my children.*
- *I am a generational curse breaker.*
- *I will not let past childhood experiences follow me into my parenting.*
- *I am showing my children affection daily.*
- *I am laying all of my burdens at the feet of God.*

Chapter 6:
Rejection

et's be honest; no one likes the feelings that come with rejection. No one wants to feel unwelcome, unappreciated, or undesired. However, in a world of free will, rejection is inevitable. How one deals with rejection is an accurate indicator of how healthy and whole that person is. Insecurities, fear, and self-doubt are derivatives of rejection. This is why it is essential to be healed and understand the depths of who you are as an individual.

If one does not have a hold on matters of the heart and she is battling internal issues such as insecurities and fears, rejection can send her into a downward spiral leading to the pits of depression.

Rejection can trigger trauma responses like those previously mentioned in Chapter 2. As a result, many relationships are compromised when one party is not able to process and cope with rejection in a healthy way.

What do I mean when I say healthy? Glad you asked. When one can deal with rejection in a healthy manner, she can see the positive in the rejection. She is able to take a step back and analyze the situation from a place of wisdom. She will ask herself questions like, "What is it that God wants me to learn from this," "What is important about this denial?" "What is the root of this rejection?"

Once these questions are processed, one can then take on a more optimistic approach in trusting that one of two things is happening. God is protecting you; God has something greater for you, and/or the denial may only be delayed. Always trust that there is protection from any rejection. Once you've taken on this perception and optimistic approach, not only can you move forward with confidence, but you can settle on the fact that greater is on the way. You've now placed your heart in a posture that is willing to release any bitterness, resentment, or ill feelings that were created from the act of being rejected. As a result, you are able to continue to walk in love despite of.

Scripture Focus:

1 Peter 2:4

"As you come to him, the living Stone-rejected by humans but chosen by God and precious to him, you also, like living stones, are being built into a spiritual house to be a holy priesthood, offering spiritual sacrifices acceptable to God through Jesus Christ."

Psalm 27:10

"Though my father and mother forsake me, the Lord will receive me."

Psalm 37:4

"Take delight in the Lord, and he will give you the desires of your heart."

With <u>faith</u> and <u>confidence</u>, declare these affirmations over your life:

- *What God has for me; it is for me.*
- *When one door closes, a better one opens.*
- *I let go of anything that is not for me.*
- *I trust that the plan that God has for my life is one that is prosperous.*
- *I will not let rejection create insecurities that will hinder my progress.*
- *I am casting all of my cares on God because he cares.*
- *God can do anything but fail.*
- *I know who I am and whose I am.*
- *I receive the rejection for my protection.*
- *I know that all things work together for those that love God.*
- *My steps are ordered by the Lord.*

Chapter 7:
Relational Codependency

R elational codependency is often described as an imbalance within a relationship where the codependent person's sense of purpose is based on making extreme sacrifices to meet their partner's needs. Codependent relationships represent a level of unhealthy behavior. This behavior is that of one who is needy and clingy.

It seems as if more women are often the codependent within relationships than men. I've seen first-hand how a woman allows another individual to dictate her happiness. Women have an innocent habit of conforming to the interests of others, whether it be partners, children, or family members. It's in our nature. Such conformity typically results in the loss of oneself. Instead of learning to be happy and whole individually, many women lean toward others to assist with her happiness...this is a major mistake. No one should have enough power to determine your level of happiness but you.

We, women, have to spend more time with God and ourselves to get to know the core of what makes us who we are. We cannot enjoy the experiences of life without knowing what we like to experience. Dating yourself is liberating. It is the only way that you can learn to authentically enjoy and be happy with yourself, *by yourself.* Happiness is a choice, and we have the power to choose joy that we can create within our own being.

Scripture Focus:

Isaiah 41:10

"So do not fear, for I am with you; do not be dismayed, for I am your God. I will strengthen you and help you; I will uphold you with my righteous right hand.

Philippians 4:13

"I can do all things through God who gives me strength."

With <u>faith</u> and <u>confidence</u>, declare these affirmations over your life:

- ◆ *I commit to myself using the same energy that I use to commit to other people.*
- ◆ *I will not depend on others when it comes to my own happiness.*

- *I attract like-minded individuals.*
- *My energy lights up the room.*
- *I love all of me.*
- *I like who I am.*
- *I will stay true to my goals and my purpose within relationships.*
- *I will not let my goals fall by the waste-side.*
- *I will create an atmosphere that is calm, relaxing, and reflective of what I desire.*
- *I will take control of my own happiness.*
- *I am allowing myself to enjoy life.*
- *I enjoy the feeling of liberation.*
- *I am free from the opinions of others.*

Chapter 8:
Healing

Healing is a word that seems to be used often nowadays. So many individuals need emotional healing. There is an entire generation that has suffered from trauma and abuse at the core of family "values" or lack thereof. As a result, we don't know how to sustain or even operate in healthy relationships. We lose sight of what it means to build others up due to insecurities derived from childhood neglect and trauma. If one does not address internal issues, the health of his or her relationships will always be at risk. Because we all know that hurt people hurt people, trauma can significantly damage relationships. One must be cognizant of his or her shortcomings and work towards healing.

Healing does not come overnight. It is an ongoing process. It can take months to many years to be healed entirely, but that should not stop anyone from pursuing healthy relationships. Healing is a journey. It is a practice and a choice where one chooses to be intentional in seeking out what causes strife within their mind, spirit, and emotions.

The goal is to seek out the root of what hinders you from being truly happy at your core and get rid of it. You cannot be your best self while carrying malice, bitterness, and anger within your heart. The process of healing requires a tremendous amount of intentionality, boundary-setting, and self-care. Once you reach the other side of your healing journey, the very act of waking up becomes joyous. There is a transformation that should take place within you holistically that causes the old you to die. A sure sign that you are making strides within your healing process is that you possess a positive energy that is undeniably pure and authentic. You want to see other people win in life, and you help celebrate the victories of others. Unhealed individuals are incapable of such genuine applause, as they seek to bring negative energy into the atmosphere in an attempt to cause a stumbling block to the healing of others. Boundaries must be set with such individuals as they cannot consume too much of your mental or physical space.

Understand that healing starts within your mind. You have to first choose to see yourself...the good and the bad. The choice to understand why and how the bad got there must also be included. Understanding is half of the battle, but once you understand your "how" and "why," accountability is now the driving force for your healing.

Scripture Focus:

1 Peter 2:24

"He himself bore our sins in his body on the cross, so that we might die to sins and live for righteousness; by his wounds you have been healed."

Psalm 41:3

"The Lord sustains them on their sickbed and restores them from their bed of illness."

Isaiah 41:10

"So do not fear, for I am with you; do not be dismayed, for I am your God."

1 Peter 5:7

"Cast all your anxiety on him because he cares for you."

With <u>faith</u> and <u>confidence</u>, declare these affirmations over your life:

- *I am healed through Christ Jesus.*
- *I give myself permission to heal.*
- *I release all negative energy that has been operating within my spirit.*
- *I release all anger, resentment, and bitterness because it is a hinderance to my healing.*
- *I am taking the necessary steps toward obtaining my healing.*
- *I have the power and authority to declare a thing into the earth.*
- *No weapon formed against me will prosper.*
- *My soul is tranquil.*
- *My thoughts are the foundation of my emotional healing.*
- *My body is always working towards perfect health.*

- *Good health is my divine right.*

- *I am receptive to God's healing power.*

- *God restores me to health and heals my wounds.*

- *I have a joyful heart because it is medicine for my soul.*

- *I will not let brokenness hinder me from functioning at my full potential.*

- *I will gird up my loins and approach the day with courage and optimism.*

Chapter 9:
Accountability

The secret to authentic healing is practicing accountability. This will be the chapter that may step on your toes, but it's ok – just say "ouch" and digest the concept. The absolute easiest thing that an individual can do is blame someone else for their pain and unfortunate circumstances. The reality is that we make choices that put us on the path of such pain and unfortunate circumstances. We choose partners, ignore red flags, mismanage finances, and some of us operate like the parents we vowed we would never be... like passing on generational curses which contribute to the misbehavior of our children. Whew! Take a minute to process and digest...inhale and exhale. We cannot expect growth without changed behavior which requires us to choose differently. Accountability requires one to examine one's own self and shortcomings.

There were quite a few times when I've had to ask myself, "What made me choose this?" or "Why am I attracted to this?" or "How did I let myself get here?" These questions are necessary when trying to determine the root of bad decision-making and overall repetitive cycles that you find yourself in. You have to get to the root of the answers to these questions to identify the cancer of why you've been operating in such a negligent way.

The moment you can identify your "why" is the moment you step into accountability and are now able to take some responsibility for your own life's decisions. True, we cannot control the decisions of others; however, we can control our own. Identifying and correcting is not only where accountability succeeds but also where healing can now begin in your life. Changed behavior can now be implemented so that evolution can take place on your behalf.

Scripture Focus:

James 5:16

"Therefore confess your sins to each other and pray for each other so that you may be healed.   The prayer of a righteous person is powerful and effective."

Romans 14:12

"So then, each of us will give an account of ourselves to God."

Proverbs 27:17

"As iron sharpens iron, so one person sharpens another."

1 Thessalonians 5:11

"Therefore encourage one another and build each other up, just as in fact you are doing."

With <u>faith</u> and <u>confidence</u>, declare these affirmations over your life:

- *I take responsibility for my own actions.*
- *I acknowledge my faults and shortcomings and make the necessary corrections needed for growth.*
- *I self-reflect often to ensure that I am living in the moment of who I am becoming.*
- *I am open to constructive criticism.*
- *I will make better choices when it comes to who I give access to in my life.*
- *I surround myself with friends that hold me responsible for my actions.*
- *I will implement changes that will accommodate the achievement of my goals.*
- *I do not blame others for my bad choices.*
- *I will own my mistakes.*
- *I will not make a permanent decision during a temporary situation.*

- *I accept the consequences of my actions.*
- *I am working on self-improvement.*
- *I am working towards becoming a better listener.*
- *I practice gratitude.*
- *I will continue to make the changes that are necessary in my life for evolution.*

It is very important that one knows who she is and what she is purposed to do on the earth. You don't know how strong you are until you've endured treacherous circumstances and have come out on top. It is not until then that you've realized your capability of enduring uncomfortable seasons throughout your life. The New Oxford American Dictionary describes resilience as the ability to withstand or recover quickly from difficult conditions. Another definition states that it is the ability to spring back into shape after being stretched or compressed. The very make-up of a woman is that of resilience.

When we consider the very act of giving

birth, we must consider the woman's ability to undergo MAXIMUM pressure, pain, and stretch. Her endurance lasts for life...literally. If you are able to maintain focus and control of your emotions during difficult times, you can overcome anything. Why? Because you are resilient!

I encourage you to meditate on the affirmations applicable to you within this read. For we know that life and death are in the power of the tongue, and when we speak things into the atmosphere, we invoke God to perform His word. As you say these affirmations aloud, say it with confidence, power, and authority. Most importantly, believe the words that are coming out of your own mouth. Trust that God will deliver on his promises. Speak life into your emotions. Approach the day with a positive attitude and a healthy mindset. Set boundaries that agree with your changed behavior, and be sure to take care of yourself at ALL costs.

Scripture Focus:

Philippians 4:8

"Finally, brothers and sisters, whatever is true, whatever is noble, whatever is right, whatever is pure, whatever is lovely, whatever is admirable-if anything is excellent or praiseworthy-think about such things. Whatever you have learned or received or heard from me or seen in me put it into practice. And the God of peace will be with you."

With <u>faith</u> and <u>confidence</u>, declare these affirmations over your life:

- ♦ *I am victorious through Christ Jesus.*
- ♦ *No weapon formed against me will prosper.*
- ♦ *I am fearfully and wonderfully made.*
- ♦ *I am a child of the most high God.*
- ♦ *All of my problems have a solution.*
- ♦ *My past pain has given me stamina to*

endure that which has been sent to destroy me.

- *I can do ALL things through Jesus Christ, who strengthens me.*
- *I am unstoppable. I am unbreakable. I am capable.*
- *I am strong.*
- *I am confident.*
- *I am a warrior.*
- *I wear my scars with pride because they signify victory.*
- *I turn pain into purpose.*
- *I am a destiny chaser.*
- *I am determined. I am driven. I am RESILIENT!*

Ashley Nicole

Ashley Nicole is a Speaker, Philanthropist, Cleric, and CEO and Founder of both Proud of You Girl Ministries, LLC and Mind Over Matter Youth Empowerment. She has created through both organizations, the capability to provide diverse groups of women with the wisdom, clarity, resources, and preparedness, quintessential for their life's excellence. Proud of You Girl Ministries, LLC functions to equip women of all ages and various walks of life, with the tools needed to activate their God-given power through the application of scripture in their daily lives, so that they may overcome life's challenges, in a healthy and holistic way. Mind Over Matter Youth Empowerment provides leadership, guidance, and the mentorship needed, in equipping teen girls with the tangible opportunity of both reshaping and developing their mindsets to grow beyond the trauma of both, past and current circumstances, into a permanent stance of victory over situational, and environmental opposition.

Ashley specializes in empowering young girls; ages 10-18, to live out their God-intentioned purpose, through a focus centered around character development, self-realization, confidence, and the cultivation of both social and life skill sets; all geared toward giving young women the inspiration to fully embrace their reality, and to initiate and maintain positive perspectives.

Ashley's Mantra is simple: She has the "gift" of experience, through which God has granted her a strong spirit of empathy not only to understand one's situation, but also to dismiss any judgment that typically coincides.

In accommodation to her incredible ethic as a servant leader, Ashley Nicole has displayed a sincere respect for higher education. She is a licensed and ordained minister and holds a Bachelor of Science from UAB, an MBA from Strayer University, and a master's in education with a concentration in Instructional Leadership. Honored greatly for her philanthropic efforts, Ashley has been awarded as an Emerging African American Leader within the Community in the southeast region and is often highlighted for the many charitable events and drives curated through her organizations.

When Ashley Nicole is not out creating better ways for humanity to function amidst the unavoidable changes of life, she is a devoted mother and friend.

Ashley Nicole. Leader. Humanitarian. Advocate.

Connect with Ashley:
Facebook: Ashley Nicole

Instagram: theeanicole_

Proud of Your Girl Ministries, LLC
Website: https://www.poyg.org

www.ingramcontent.com/pod-product-compliance
Lightning Source LLC
Chambersburg PA
CBHW060349130626
46553CB00003B/1152